Walking with Peter:
following the Way
when you can't see the path

A.J. Kilbourn

2 following the Way

Other books by A.J. Kilbourn:

<u>Novels</u>
The Prophecy (Book 1 of Sons of Tundyel)
Hindsight

<u>Christian Life</u>
Do you know how loved you are? (children's book)
Glimpses of His Magnificence: A Study of God's Power
(devotional)

***

To learn more about the author, visit
lifefaithful.blogspot.com

To contact the author, email
ajkilbourn.ajk@gmail.com

All Scriptures are from the Holy Bible, NIV, unless otherwise noted.

ISBN-13: 978-1508635253 (CreateSpace-Assigned)
ISBN-10: 1508635250

For you, the one struggling to find the path.
Because I'm right there with you.
~AJK

6 following the Way

a note from the author.

There's just something about Simon Peter that makes him stand out to me. When I read his story, somehow I see myself in him.

I don't know what it is—maybe I identify with his stubbornness and impulsiveness or something—but I'm drawn into his story in a way I'm not pulled into anyone else's.

Mostly, though, I think what I like most about Peter's story is that he doesn't come across as having a perfect, unshakable faith. The thing about Peter is, he never seems to know what's coming next yet he still runs forward at full speed. Sometimes this leads to him stumbling, but when he falls he always know what to do—he cries, "Lord, save me!"

That's where I find myself lately. I have no idea what's in front of me, but I'm running full speed ahead, plowing down what so often seems like a path in the dark.

If you're there, maybe you'll identify with Peter, too.

Week 1

Week 1: monday

"As Jesus walked beside the Sea of Galilee, He saw Simon and his brother Andrew casting a net into the lake, for they were fishermen. 'Come, follow Me,' Jesus said, 'and I will make you fishers of men.' At once they left their nets and followed Him."

~Mark 1:16-18

***

Though it's not entirely clear from this passage, these two brothers didn't drop everything to follow some random stranger. That would have made their story a bit odd, and I think I would have to wonder about two guys who thought it would be fun to go fishing for men!

Thankfully, there's a bit of a back story that tells us Andrew was a disciple of John the Baptist, Jesus's cousin and the man who pointed Him out as the Messiah the Jewish people were waiting for. Still, though, the fact that they had been *sort of* introduced doesn't make their decision to simply follow Jesus any less incredible.

Because, you see, while it's a simple thing to follow Christ, it's not an easy thing.

I say it's a simple thing because all it takes is belief that Jesus is the Messiah. That doesn't make it easy, though.

For Peter (called Simon here, but we'll talk about that tomorrow), walking away from his nets wouldn't have been easy. At one point, we're told about Peter's mother-in-law being healed—which means he had a wife. Think about that for a minute. Peter had a wife at home, so after he and his brother decided to follow Jesus he had to go home and tell his wife. Can you hear how that conversation might have started? "Well, I don't have my nets, because this guy walked by and me and Andrew left everything sitting there because He told us He was going to have us fish for men...No, I haven't lost my mind, I'm just..."

Making the decision to follow Christ means leaving other things behind. It's not always an easy thing to do, but it's worth it because it's life changing in unimaginable ways.

week 1: tuesday

"Jesus looked at him and said, 'You are Simon son of John. You will be called Cephas.'"

~John 1:42

***

I wonder how it would feel to know the name God has for me. In Revelation 2:17 we are told that we will receive a new name one day, a true name that tells who we are to God. Here, Simon got to know his name right off the bat: Cephas, or Peter as we know him.

Cephas has an interesting meaning: rock. Here's Jesus, telling Simon that his new name will be one that speaks to how solid and steady he is. As we work our way through Peter's walk with Christ, hold onto that thought. Before anything else happened in Peter's life, Jesus named him Cephas, the rock. There is no doubt in my mind that even then Jesus knew what Peter would face. He knew Peter's faith would be shaky at times, and that sometimes his impulsiveness would get the best of him, but that didn't change the name He had for Peter.

When I look at my own life, most of the time what stands out to me are all the ways I feel like I've failed to live up to the amazing gift of being called a child of God. I see my temper, my over-sensitivity, my stubbornness, my procrastination. I see my fears and doubts that surface even though I know all the "Sunday school answers," and I wonder how much my faltering faith hurts God.

Despite all my faults (or maybe partly because of them), God has a name for me. It's not the name I would pick for myself, I'm sure, because it's the name that speaks to who I truly am. All those faults I listed? I struggle with them on a daily basis, and I have to ask God's forgiveness for things related to them all the time. But the beautiful thing is, all those things have been covered by the overwhelming, all-encompassing presence of Christ, and He sees me with a new name.

notes:

week 1: wednesday

"When the disciples saw Him walking on the lake, they were terrified. 'It's a ghost,' they said, and cried out in fear.

But Jesus immediately said to them: 'Take courage! It is I. Don't be afraid.'

'Lord, if it's You,' Peter replied, 'tell me to come to You on the water.'

'Come,' He said.

Then Peter got down out of the boat, walked on the water and came toward Jesus. But when he saw the wind, he was afraid and, beginning to sink, cried out, 'Lord, save me!'

Immediately, Jesus reached out His hand and caught him. 'You of little faith,' He said, 'why did you doubt?'

~Matthew 14:26-31

***

Here, we get to see Peter's impulsiveness. I mean, who else would have told Jesus to have him walk on the water? We also get to see two very different pictures of Peter's faith.

First, there's the guy who stepped out of the boat. Peter knew what he was asking was impossible by human standards. There is no one in his right mind who would step out of a boat expecting to walk along on top of the water. After all, that's the whole reason we need boats.

Yet, despite the fact that it was impossible, all it took was one word from Jesus to get Peter to step out of the boat.

And then there he was, doing the impossible as he walked towards Jesus on top of the water.

It think it was right about then that Peter's logical mind caught up with what was happening. That side of him saw how the wind was tossing the waves, and it started *reasoning.* That side started overshadowing the part of him that had stepped out in a show of childlike faith, faith that said he could do the impossible as long as Jesus was calling him. In that moment, Peter—the one Jesus had named Cephas, the rock—was shaken. His faith seemed far away, and he was sinking.

But then, Peter did the only thing that mattered: he cried out, "Lord, save me!"

And you know the incredible thing? Matthew tells us that Jesus *immediately* saved him. He didn't lecture Peter on his faltering faith until after He had pulled him up to His side.

Sometimes, God asks us to do something that seems, for all practical purposes, impossible. In my own life, there have been many times when I've stepped out of the boat and then noticed the storm raging around me. Where I'm different from Peter, though, is that when I start to sink I start trying to work things out for myself. I desperately tread water, gasping for air while the waves crash over me.

How much better would it be if I would cry out, "Lord, save me!" when I first start sinking? Instead, sometimes I wait so long to ask for help that Jesus has to dive under to pull me back up. I can hear Him asking me, "You of little faith, why did you doubt?"

notes:

week 1: thursday

"When Jesus came to the region of Caesarea Philippi, He asked His disciples, 'Who do people say the Son of Man is?'

They replied, 'Some say John the Baptist; others say Elijah; and still others, Jeremiah or one of the prophets.'

'But what about you?' He asked. 'Who do you say I am?'

Simon Peter answered, 'You are the Christ, the Son of the living God.'"

~Matthew 16:13-16

***

Who do people say Jesus is? That question is just as big today as it was the day Jesus asked His disciples. For a while, some people simply tried to argue that Jesus wasn't real. I think one reason for that was that as long as He wasn't real, people could ignore His teachings without feeling guilty. Whatever the reason for the argument, that's not as common today. Too many historians outside of those who recorded the Bible have documented the existence of Jesus, a rebel preacher from Nazareth.

So today, people usually resort to saying, "Jesus was just a good man whose teachings help you live a good life." In Jesus's own day, the answer wasn't much different. People were saying that perhaps He was a prophet. They acknowledged that His teachings were from God, but that was about it.

In this passage, we get another glimpse of Peter's impetuousness. This time, though, it's in a good way. When Jesus turned the question toward His disciples, it was Peter who spoke up and said, "You are the Christ, the Son of the living God."

Peter's answer wasn't popular. It didn't fit with the cautious manner in which most people were regarding Jesus.

Instead, his quick answer was a simple statement of faith. He wasn't worried about what anyone else would think.

In today's world, it's not popular to say that Jesus is the Christ, the Messiah, the Son of the One True God. That sets Him in a position of supremacy and authority, and those are two positions people don't want to give to only one person. The world wants to say that while Jesus is a good example to follow, He is not the only way. The trouble with that is that Jesus Himself said, "I am the way and the truth and the life. No one comes to the Father except through Me." (John 14:6)

To say that Jesus is the Way is not popular, but we should be more worried about *pleasing God* with our words than pleasing the world. Don't be afraid to say, "You are the Christ, the Son of the living God."

week 1: friday

"From that time on Jesus began to explain to His disciples that He must go to Jerusalem and suffer many things at the hands of the elders, chief priests, and teachers of the law, and that He must be killed and on the third day be raised to life.

   Peter took Him aside and began to rebuke Him. 'Never, Lord!' he said. 'This shall never happen to you!'

   Jesus turned and said to Peter, 'Get behind me, Satan! You are a stumbling block to me; you do not have in mind the things of God, but the things of men.'"

~Matthew 16:21-23

* * *

Sometimes, even Jesus's closest friends—the Twelve—had a hard time coming to terms with what He told them. That's the case here, where Jesus was trying to explain to His disciples that He wouldn't be staying with them. They apparently weren't getting it the subtle way, so Jesus was blunt and told them He had to be killed and raised back to life.

At that time, I don't think the whole "brought back to life" thing registered with the Twelve. They were a bit hung up on the killing part, and understandably so. To many of the Jewish people, the Messiah was seen as a warrior who would free them from oppression by foreign powers, someone who would crush the enemy and establish an earthly kingdom for Israel. The disciples were starting to see Jesus as the Messiah, so Him being killed didn't fit in with their plans.

That's when Peter's quick mouth shows up again. Matthew tells us that Peter pulled Jesus aside and rebuked Him.

The word for rebuke is from the Greek root "epiplesso,"

meaning to strike at. That takes some nerve, doesn't it? Peter didn't calmly and quietly ask Jesus to clarify. He struck out with his words, arguing with Jesus.

I wouldn't even want to start listing off all the times I've argued with God, telling Him just what I though of His plans. For some strange reason (stubbornness? Independence?), I get this thought in my head that *my* way is best, that I know better than God how my life should be mapped out.

Jesus's answer to Peter wasn't so calm and quiet, either. He said, "Get behind me, Satan! You are a stumbling block to Me; you do not have in mind the things of God, but the things of men."

It makes me wonder, how many times have I made myself a stumbling block, putting myself in the way of God's plan simply because my perspective is wrong? One thing's for sure, it's more times than I care to admit (and probably more times than I realize).

God's plans aren't our plans. He sees the big picture when all we can see is one tiny, blurry piece of the puzzle. Though giving up my desire for control is an issue I'm still working on, it is comforting to know that God is always in control.

notes:

Week 2

week 2: monday

"Then Peter came to Jesus and asked, 'Lord, how many times shall I forgive my brother when he sins against me? Up to seven times?'

   Jesus answered, 'I tell you, not seven times, but seventy times seven.'"

~Matthew 18:21-22

***

I think it's interesting that Peter tacked on "when he sins against me" to his question about forgiveness. It's like he's wanting to make sure that Jesus realizes he's asking about when he's been wronged, not just when there's been a misunderstanding and hurt feelings. Peter was a straightforward guy, so he wanted a straightforward answer. He figured it was more than the three times the rabbis taught, so he went with seven. It was the perfect number, after all, so surely that was the answer Jesus would give.

I think Jesus pretty much blew him out of the water with His answer of seventy times seven. I have to admit, the idea of forgiving someone 490 times isn't something I'm super excited about, either—especially considering the clarification that we're talking about something more than misunderstandings!

I've been in that place before. Like Peter, I've asked God a question with an answer in mind. Surely He'll confirm what I think, because I've put a lot of thought into it and I've come up with a pretty good answer. What I've found is that most of the time I'm blown away when I get an answer I didn't expect, something I never could have imagined. Sometimes, like Peter being told to forgive his brother not seven times, but seventy times seven, the answer is something I don't like.

That's when it's important to back track a bit, to remember that my ways aren't God's ways and that I'm not seeing the full path laid out ahead of me.

notes:

week 2: tuesday

"Jesus knew that the Father had put all things under His power, and that He had come from God and was returning to God; so He got up from the meal, took off His outer clothing, and wrapped a towel around His waist. After that, He poured water into a basin and began to wash His disciples feet, drying them with the towel that was wrapped around Him.

   He came to Simon Peter, who said to Him, 'Lord, are You going to wash my feet?'

   Jesus replied, 'You do not realize now what I am doing, but later you will understand.'

   'No,' said Peter, 'You shall never wash my feet.'

   Jesus answered, 'Unless I wash you, you have no part with me.'

   'Then, Lord,' Simon Peter replied, 'not just my feet but my hands and my head as well!'"

~John 13:3-9

***

Right about now is when my people in the South would probably start saying, "That Peter, bless his heart..." Again, Peter is arguing with Jesus. They were at the Passover Seder, and Jesus started to wash His disciples' feet. I'm sure the other disciples thought it was strange, too, but from what we're told it's only Peter who speaks up.

He questions Jesus's actions. He doesn't understand what's being done, but he knows he's not worthy of having Jesus act as his servant.

His questioning isn't wrong. Does it surprise you to hear that? So often we're taught that we should never question God, but I think He understands our questions. He knows that we can't see what He sees, and that we just don't understand. I think He's more than big enough to handle our questions.

That's not to say that He will give us a direct answer to our questions, though. Sometimes He may, but more often than not it seems like His answers come to us in the form that Jesus gave Peter: "This is how I'm doing things, and if you want to be part of what I'm doing you're going to have to go along with it."

Peter, being Peter, jumped right in then, asking Jesus to wash all of him if that's what it would take to belong to Him. Sometimes, faith means jumping in when it doesn't make sense just because that's what God has asked you to do. It means allowing Him to work even when you can't understand what He's doing, knowing that that's what it takes to belong with Him.

 notes:

week 2: wednesday

"Simon Peter asked Him, 'Lord, where are you going?'
  Jesus replied, 'Where I am going, you cannot follow now, but you will follow later.'
  Peter asked, 'Lord, why can't I follow You now? I will lay down my life for you.'
  Then Jesus answered, 'Will you really lay down your life for Me? I tell you the truth, before the rooster crows, you will disown me three times!'"

~John 13:36-38

***

It seems like Peter had developed quite the habit of talking back to Jesus, huh? Here, following the last Passover Jesus celebrated with His disciples, He was explaining to them that He was about to have to leave them. I guess since the blunt approach hadn't gotten things across to them, He decided to try the subtle route again.

Blunt or subtle, Peter's reaction to Jesus's words stays pretty much the same--"Wait, I would die for you, so I'm going, too!"

I guess we can say one thing for him—his response has improved. Just a little while earlier, Peter was arguing with Jesus, telling Him that there was no way he would let Jesus be killed. He must have learned something from Jesus calling him Satan, because here he changes his answer a bit. Instead of telling Jesus that he won't let Him be killed, Peter says he will die with Him.

He may be hot-headed and impetuous, but Peter's also deeply committed to Christ.

The thing is, sometimes even our commitment isn't enough to keep us on the straight and narrow. Sometimes, even our best intentions fall short.

Peter—Cephas, the rock—was told that not only was he going to deny Christ, he was going to do so three times before the rooster crowed in the morning.

I'm sure Peter thought there was no chance of that. They had just finished the Passover Seder, a joyous occasion. Not only was it crazy to think that he would deny Jesus, I don't imagine Peter thought there would even be a situation that night where the possibility could come up.

My own life has unfolded *much* differently than I would ever have imagined. There have been times when I felt utterly abandoned by God, times when I cried out to Him in unbelievable anger and anguish. If I had been told as a teenager that those moments would come, I'm pretty sure I wouldn't have believed it.

What about you? Have you had those moments?

 notes:

week 2: thursday

"'Simon, Simon, Satan has asked to sift you as wheat. But I have prayed for you, Simon, that your faith may not fail. And when you have turned back, strengthen your brothers.'"

~Luke 22:31-32

***

Yesterday, we looked at John's account of when Jesus predicted Peter's denial. Here we have Luke's addition. Peter was confident that he would take a stand for Jesus no matter what, even if it meant that he would have to die. The thing is, that's not what was in store for Peter.

Satan wanted to "sift [Peter] as wheat." Basically, that meant he wanted to run him through the wringer and beat him up a bit to see if Peter really meant it when he said he was a follower of Christ. From my point of view, it would have been really great to read that Jesus said something along the lines of, "But I told him that he doesn't get to cause you any trouble, so you can look forward to a long, happy life following Me."

But that's not what He said.

Instead, Jesus basically said, "I'm going to let him put you through some hard stuff." Jesus knew Peter would deny Him. He even knew how many times and when it would happen. He knew that Peter's faith would be shaken: his faith in Christ and his faith in his own ability to follow Him. Jesus knows all the hard times you've gone through and what you'll go through in the future. None of it is a surprise to Him. What's amazing, though, is that Jesus didn't just know what Peter would face; He prayed for Peter. He knew exactly what to pray for, too.

Jesus prayed for all of us, but to take it even a step further we're told in Romans 8:26 that the Holy Spirit prays for us when we don't know how to pray for ourselves.

Jesus could have stopped there. After all, knowing that Jesus had prayed for him probably would have been enough to keep Peter going through the hard times. But God doesn't stop at "just enough." He "is able to do exceeding abundantly above all that we ask or think" (Ephesians 3:20 KJV).

So Jesus added one more sentence, a promise for Peter to cling to and a challenge for him to live up to: "And when you have turned back, strengthen your brothers." The promise was that Peter would come back to his faith. The challenge was for him to use his own hard times and rough experiences to help others.

It would be so much easier if we were promised that we would never face hard times that tested our faith, but that's not the case. Instead, we have the same assurance that Jesus gave Peter—He has prayed for us. When we are in the middle of the dark, hard times, we need to hold fast to that promise and remember the challenge that goes along with it.

notes:

week 2: friday

"Then He said to them, 'My soul is overwhelmed with sorrow to the point of death. Stay here and keep watch with Me.'

Going a little farther, He fell with His face to the ground and prayed. 'My Father, if it is possible, may this cup be taken from Me. Yet not as I will, but as You will.'

Then He returned to His disciples and found them sleeping. 'Could you men not keep watch with Me for one hour?' He asked Peter. 'Watch and pray so that you will not fall into temptation. The spirit is willing, but the body is weak.'

He went away a second time and prayed, 'My Father, if it is not possible for this cup to be taken away unless I drink it, may Your will be done.'

When He came back, He again found them sleeping, because their eyes were heavy. So He left them and went away once more and prayed the third time, saying the same thing.

Then He returned to the disciples and said to them, 'Are you still sleeping and resting? Look, the hour is near, and the Son of Man is betrayed into the hands of sinners.'"

~Matthew 26:38-45

***

Events that night were unfolding in a way none of the disciples could have imagined. After their dinner, Jesus went to the garden to pray. He pulled Peter, James, and John a little further along than the rest, asking them to keep watch for Him.

This wasn't a typical prayer. When Jesus prayed that night, His prayer was so long that the disciples fell asleep three times when they were supposed to be keeping watch. Jesus was in anguish, a kind of anguish we can never understand.

Yet, in the midst of His own dark night, Jesus made it a point to make it a teachable moment for Peter. Remember, Jesus knew what the rest of the night would hold for Peter. He knew that Peter was about to deny Him; He knew how much Peter's faith was about to be shaken. So He told Peter, "Watch and pray so that you will not fall into temptation. The spirit is willing, but the body is weak."

God knows our hearts. He knows our intentions, but He also knows that we are human. He sees our weaknesses and knows that from time to time they manage to drown out our faith.

Week 3

week 3: monday

"Then Simon Peter, who had a sword, drew it and struck
the high priest's servant, cutting off his right ear."

~John 18:10

***

The night had just taken a drastic change. Jesus had just
been betrayed with a kiss from Judas, one of the Twelve
who they had all called a friend. Now, a mob was there
insisting on arresting Jesus. The quiet of the night had been
interrupted by men carrying torches, lanterns, and
weapons (John 18:3).

Peter was true to his word. He was ready to fight to protect
Jesus, and his impulsive side took control. I imagine that
made the situation pretty tense; both sides were likely
ready for things to spin out of control.

What would it have been like to see Jesus right then, to
watch Him calmly reach out and heal the servant's ear
(Luke 22:51)?

I imagine the disciples were terrified. This wasn't what was
supposed to happen, at least not in their plan. Yet in the
middle of the chaos, Jesus showed very plainly that He was
still in control.

Peter's actions could have gotten him in a lot of trouble. He
thought he was doing something for Jesus, but actually he
was just causing more trouble. Again, his actions serve as a
reminder that we don't see the whole picture. Our plans
aren't the same as God's plans.

In the middle of the chaos, when the quiet of the night is

interrupted by men with weapons—whether those are literal weapons or verbal weapons—God is still in control. He is not surprised by what we've gotten into, and He's right there in the mess with us, ready to bring healing to what we've messed up.

notes:

week 3: tuesday

"The Lord turned and looked straight at Peter. Then Peter remembered the word the Lord had spoken to him: 'Before the rooster crows today, you will disown me three times.' And he went outside and wept bitterly."

Luke 22:61-62

***

Peter had failed his Lord.

After Jesus was arrested, Peter followed the mob that was leading Him to the high priest's house. Three times, people pointed out that Peter was a follower of Christ, and each time Peter's answer was that he didn't know what they were talking about. The third time he was denying even so much as knowing Jesus, the rooster crowed.

He hadn't been strong enough to stand up and even admit a connection with Christ, let alone die with Him.

Jesus was right in the middle of His ultimate trial, yet as the rooster crowed He took the time to look at Peter. He saw Peter, even then in the middle of His arrest and questioning.

I can only imagine what Peter saw in those eyes at that moment. Here was his best friend, the One he had given up everything to follow. Just earlier that night he had promised to be faithful even if it meant death, and here he was saying he didn't even know who Jesus was.

I'm pretty sure Peter's faith was in the dirt at that moment. He had failed Jesus, and he knew that Jesus knew it.

As much as it pains me to admit it, I've been there. My faith has been in the dirt, trampled by my own actions or lack of actions. I've failed God by not taking a stand when I should have, and in those moments I've been reminded by just how much I've hurt my Lord because He saw my denial of Him.

It's a pretty horrible place to be.

week 3: wednesday

"So Peter and the other disciple started for the tomb. Both were running, but the other disciple reached the tomb first. He bent over and looked in at the strips of linen laying there but did not go in. Then Simon Peter, who was behind him, arrived and went into the tomb. He saw the strips of linen lying there, as well as the burial cloth that had been around Jesus's head. The cloth was folded up by itself, separate from the linen. Finally the other disciple, who had reached the tomb first, also went inside. He saw and believed. (They still did not understand from Scripture that Jesus had to rise from the dead.)"

~John 20:3-9

***

When Mary Magdalene told them that Jesus's body was gone, Peter and John hurried to the tomb. John couldn't bring himself to go inside at first, but Peter didn't hesitate. He went into the open tomb to see where Jesus had been placed.

Peter was desperate for Jesus.

His faith had faltered, but that didn't mean it was gone.

Jesus's death was a dark moment for His followers. They couldn't see what was going to happen, no matter how many times He had spelled everything out for them. All they could see was the darkness, and they were lost in despair.

We face dark times, too, those times when it seems like the world has crashed down around us.

It's in those times that it is so important that we hold out hope for Jesus. Even faced with what seems like the worst news, we should run to Jesus. Like Peter, we should be desperate for Him, so desperate that we are willing to even run into the tomb in search of Him.

We won't always find Him. Like Peter and John, we may run into the place we expect to find Jesus only to be surprised that He isn't there. The thing is, when He isn't where we expect to find Him, that's usually because He's planning on meeting us somewhere so much better.

 notes:

week 3: thursday

"Then the disciple whom Jesus loved said to Peter, 'It is the Lord!' As soon as Simon Peter heard him say, 'It is the Lord,' he wrapped his outer garment around him (for he had taken it off) and jumped into the water."

~John 21:7

***

In a way, we've come full circle with this verse. Peter and some of the other disciples were out fishing on the Sea of Galilee. We're told a couple verses later that they were about 100 yards from the shore. Apparently they spent the night out on the water and didn't catch anything. The next morning, some man on the shore told them to throw their nets out on the other side of the boat.

Let's stop right there for a minute. Here's this group of guys, men who know what they're doing out on a fishing boat. They've been fishing all night, and yet they still toss out the nets again when some man on the shore tells them to. Talk about optimism!

To be fair, though, this is after Jesus had appeared to them in a locked room (John 20:24-30). They had seen Jesus arrested, beaten, crucified, buried—and resurrected. I guess after all that, they had every reason to be optimistic.

It was John who recognized Jesus on the shore—but it was Peter who jumped into the water to go to Him.

Peter still hurried to Jesus.

Despite the fact that he had denied even so much as knowing Jesus the night He was arrested, Peter had no doubt that Jesus would accept him fully and welcome him ashore with open arms.

When we deny the One who saved us, it hurts Him more than we can imagine. When we turn back to Him, though—when we dive out of the boat in our desperation to get back to Him—He welcomes us. He doesn't hold our betrayal against us. Instead, as we'll look at tomorrow, He forgives us completely.

 notes:

week 3: friday

"When they had finished eating, Jesus said to Simon Peter, 'Simon, son of John, do you truly love Me more than these?'

'Yes, Lord,' he said, 'You know that I love You.'

Jesus said, 'Feed my lambs.'

Again Jesus said, 'Simon, son of John, do you truly love Me?'

He answered, 'Yes, Lord, You know that I love You.'

Jesus said, 'Take care of My sheep.'

The third time He said to him, 'Simon, son of John, do you love Me?'

Peter was hurt because Jesus asked him the third time, 'Do you love Me?' He said, 'Lord, You know all things; You know that I love You.'

Jesus said, 'Feed My sheep.'"

John 21:15-17

***

Three times, Peter had denied Christ. Three times, he had said that he didn't even know the man. And here, three times, Jesus let Peter confirm his love.

Peter obviously didn't get what was going on at the time, or I don't think he would have gotten hurt when Jesus asked him that third time. With what we know of Peter, though, I imagine a little later it clicked and he thought, "Ah, now I get what He was doing there!" Undoubtedly, it would have humbled him to see just how far Jesus went to make sure Peter knew he was forgiven.

Just like when Jesus looked straight at Peter in the midst of the chaos of His own arrest, God sees us when we hurt Him. He sees how much it hurts us when we realize that we've failed Him. That's why He gives us the chance to repent, to confirm that we love Him despite our failure.

There's a saying: "The Devil's in the details." I think it's a lot more fitting to say that "God's in the details." He's intricately involved with every aspect of our lives. It's hard to imagine, but the One who sees the big picture is also the One who works out the tiny details. Just like with Peter, He goes to great lengths to make sure we understand that He forgives us—that He loves us.

Sometimes, it's not until we look back later that we can say, "Ah, now I get what He was doing there!"

Week 4

week 4: monday

"Peter turned and saw that the disciple whom Jesus loved was following them. (This was the one who had leaned back against Jesus at the supper and had said, 'Lord, who is going to betray You?') When Peter saw him, he asked, 'Lord, what about him?'

Jesus answered, 'If I want him to remain alive until I return, what is that to you? You must follow me.'"

~John 21:20-22

***

After giving Peter three chances to confirm his love, Jesus went on to tell him some things Peter didn't really want to hear. He told Peter to follow Him, even when it meant letting people lead him where he didn't want to go.

Apparently, this didn't set so well with Peter. That's when he noticed John. Maybe things wouldn't go so perfectly for him, either. Misery loves company, right? So Peter, maybe hoping to make himself feel better by hearing that somebody else might not like what was in store, asked Jesus, "what about him?"

Isn't it easy to do that sometimes? You see all the stuff going on in your own life and think that surely you can't be the only one. Maybe it would feel better to know that somebody else was having a rough time, too.

Here's the hard answer: Jesus basically told Peter to mind his own business. He told Peter that it didn't matter what was in store for somebody else because He expected Peter to follow Him, no matter what.

We shouldn't be focused on God's plans for other believers.

We shouldn't feel slighted because it seems like someone else has greater blessings in store, or because their lives seem easier. We have one task: to follow Christ. No matter what, that is what He expects from us.

I think it's interesting to note that the first and last recorded words directly from Jesus to Peter were "Follow Me." No qualifications or clarifications, just a simple command.

Follow Me.

 notes:

week 4: tuesday

"Men of Israel, listen to this: Jesus of Nazareth was a man accredited by God to you by miracles, wonders, and signs, which God did among you through Him, as you yourselves know. This man was handed over to you by God's set purpose and foreknowledge; and you, with the help of wicked men, put Him to death by nailing Him to the cross. But God raised Him from the dead, freeing Him from the agony of death, because it was impossible for death to keep its hold on Him."

~Acts 2:22-24

***

Once, Jesus told Peter that Satan has asked to sift him like wheat. Do you remember that? Jesus gave Peter a challenge that day—He told him that He had prayed for Peter to keep his faith, and He told Peter to strengthen his brothers once he had turned back.

Peter went through a major crisis of faith. He was shaken, most likely to the very core of his being. He even went so far as to deny knowing Jesus.

But God.

God held Peter through it all, and brought him through stronger on the other side, just as Jesus had promised that day.

Peter went on to speak boldly for Christ, even though it wasn't the safe or popular thing to do. He spent the rest of his life trying his best to live up to the challenge Jesus had given him.

When your faith is shaken, know that God is waiting for you. Just as Christ's death had a set purpose and was done with God's foreknowledge, so is whatever trial you're going through. When you turn back, strengthen your brothers.

notes:

week 4: wednesday

"They had Peter and John brought before them and began to question them: 'By what power or what name did you do this?'

   Then Peter, filled with the Holy Spirit, said to them: 'Rulers and elders of the people! If we are being called to account today for an act of kindness shown to a cripple and are asked how he was healed, then know this, you and all the people of Israel: It is by the name of Jesus Christ of Nazareth, whom you crucified but whom God raised from the dead, that this man stands before you healed. He is "the stone you builders rejected, which has become the capstone." Salvation is found in no one else, for there is no other name under heaven given to men by which we must be saved.'

Acts 4:7-12

***

Peter and John were tossed into jail for what they were preaching, particularly that Jesus rose from the dead and that through Him, eternal life was available to all who believed. The next day, they were called before all the religious leaders, men who had spent their lives studying the Law and the Scriptures. Peter and John were fishermen, so for most people in their position this would have been the perfect time to just be quiet. For Peter, though, that just doesn't seem to be an option.

Once again, his impulsiveness and lack of fear kick in—this time, aided by the Holy Spirit. Peter starts telling the high priests about Jesus. He wasn't just telling them about the man, either, though pointing out all the wonderful things Jesus did for people before He was killed would have been quite a list. Instead, he says something the high priests didn't want to hear: "Salvation is found in no one else, for there is no other name under heaven given to men by which we must be saved."

That's a bold statement, but even though Peter knew they wouldn't want to hear what he had to say, he wasn't afraid to speak out. In today's world, people still don't want to hear that Jesus is the only way to salvation. Many people preach tolerance, saying that as long as we are all trying to be *good people*, we are all working toward Heaven. The thing is, we are told over and over again in the Bible that that's not the case. Being a *good person* has nothing to do with it, because none of us could ever be good enough to earn our way into Heaven. Salvation is a gift, paid for by the blood of Christ, and available only to those who follow Him as the Way.

It's easy not to feel qualified to stand up and speak the truth. We look at those around us and feel like we shouldn't be speaking up. I've heard it said before that, "God doesn't call the qualified, He qualifies the called." We have a clear picture of that here. Peter wasn't qualified to speak to the high priests on matters of religion. Yet, because of his walk with Christ, he had the Holy Spirit on his side and the high priests were astonished by his words.

We're told at the end of verse 13, "they took note that these men had been with Jesus." No matter what other qualifications you may or may not have, when people look at your life do they know that you have been with Jesus?

notes:

week 4: thursday

"Praise be to the God and Father of our Lord Jesus Christ!
In His great mercy He has given us new birth into a living
hope through the resurrection of Jesus Christ from the
dead, and into an inheritance that can never perish, spoil,
or fade—kept in heaven for you, who through faith are
shielded by God's power until the coming of the salvation
that is ready to be revealed in the last time. In this you
greatly rejoice, though now for a little while you may have
had to suffer grief in all kinds of trials. These have come so
that your faith—of greater worth than gold, which perishes
even though refined by fire—may be proved genuine and
may result in praise, glory, and honor when Jesus Christ is
revealed. Though you have not seen Him, you love Him;
and even though you do not see Him now, you believe in
Him and are filled with an inexpressible and glorious joy, for
you are receiving the goal of your faith, the salvation of
your souls."

I Peter 1:3-9

***

These last couple of days, I want to look at some of Peter's
words from one of his letters. When Peter got the challenge
from Jesus to strengthen his brothers, I don't think he had
any idea what was about to happen. Once that crisis of
faith had passed, though, Peter did just what he had been
told to do. He focused his life on telling others about Christ
and teaching them how to strengthen their faith.

When you answer "yes" to Jesus, you have no idea where
it's going to take you or what you're going to go through.
There's something you can count on, though—it's not
always going to be easy. As followers of Christ, we aren't
promised a smooth road. Instead, we are promised that
Jesus will be with us through everything we face, even
during those dark times when we can't see Him.

Peter faced the darkest night of his life knowing that Jesus had been taken from him, and that he had denied his Lord. That night, he was filled with grief for his loss. What he had lost sight of, though, was that once we have started walking with Christ, we are never abandoned. There's a quote I heard once that says, "Jesus didn't come to get you out of trouble, but rather to get into it with you." I've long ago forgotten the speaker's name, but his words have earned a coveted spot on the once blank pages inside the front cover of my Bible. Jesus is there, even when we can't see Him— right in the middle of the troubles we face.

week 4: friday

"Humble yourselves, therefore, under God's mighty hand, that He may lift you up in due time. Cast all your anxiety on Him because He cares for you.

Be self-controlled and alert. Your enemy the devil prowls around like a roaring lion looking for someone to devour. Resist him, standing firm in the faith, because you know that your brothers throughout the world are undergoing the same kind of sufferings."

~I Peter 5:6-9

***

Perhaps one of the most beautiful lessons we can learn from Peter—this hard headed, impetuous, fast-talking, quick tempered disciple—is that God cares for us. He sees us when we feel alone in the dark, and He watches as we grope around trying to find the path on our own. The whole time, He is waiting for us to look to Him.

Sometimes, the darkness is Satan's way of trying to "sift you as wheat." He wants to shake you, because by doing that he can keep you from walking the path God has laid out for you. Just remember that you aren't alone in the dark. Like Peter said, stand firm in your faith and in the knowledge that Jesus has walked through that darkness, too. He knows the sorrow and temptation well, and He has prayed for you.

"And the God of all grace, who called you to His eternal glory in Christ, after you have suffered a little while, will Himself restore you and make you strong, firm, and steadfast. To Him be the power for ever and ever. Amen."

~I Peter 5:10-11

notes:

Made in the USA
Columbia, SC
20 February 2023

12611486R00026